INDIANS
OF THE
NORTHWEST

Stan Garrod

Fitzhenry & Whiteside

INDIANS OF THE NORTHWEST
©1994,1986, Fitzhenry & Whiteside Limited

Canadian Cataloguing in Publication Data

Garrod, Stan
   Indians of the Northwest Coast

(First Nations Series -
   Inside Communities)

ISBN 0-88902-086-8 pa.

1. Indians of North America - Northwest coast
of North America. I. Title. II. Series.

E78.N78G37   970'.004'97   C79-094441-3

Table of Contents

Acknowledgements

Editors: Ian Gillen
                  Nicholas Stephens

Designer: Arne Roosman

Printed in Canada

Photograph and Picture credits:

Acorn Art   7,8,20,22,24,28,32,35,36,37,38
American Museum of Natural History   16
BC Department of Travel & Tourism   24,60,61
BC Provincial Archives   3,10,16,17,18,21,25,26,27,28,29,31,34,
35,49,54,55,59
BC Provincial Museum   11,12-13,20,21,27,32,33,51,52,56,58,62
British Museum   23
CN Photography   15
Glenbow Museum   19
National Museums of Canada   10,11,32,43,46
Oregon Historical Society   29
Public Archives Canada   21,23,27,58
Royal Ontario Museum   5,19,47
Smithsonian Institution   50
Stark Museum   44

INTRODUCTION

An old woman sat in front of the classroom. Her grandson stood beside her, beating a drum softly so as to not drown out her soft but musical voice. The students sat silently, fascinated as the woman with the wise and weathered brown face spoke to them:

> Do you know about Raven? Raven is the trickster, a practical joker. And Raven is the creator, the clever one who brings the berries to feed them. All of the old peoples of the Pacific Coast knew about Raven. Raven, he was so famous that his stories were carried all over the place. Why, even the Inuit people and the people of the prairies knew about Raven. That's how important he was...

Among the students sitting in front of the story teller was Paul Bedard. Paul's family had just moved from New Brunswick to Bella Coola and this was the first time he had ever heard a native story teller. Her voice was so soft that he had to strain to hear, but her words carried him away to another time and place.

Raven was always attracted by shiny things. If you look closely you'll see that, even today, ravens like to pick up shiny bits of tin foil or metal from the ground and carry them away. Well, one day, Raven looked up in the sky and he saw something shiny, so bright and shiny that he knew he had to have it. That's right, Raven wanted to steal the sun from the sky.

Eagle watched Raven looking at the sun and laughed. "I am the most powerful bird in the sky world, Raven," said Eagle. "If any bird can take the sun from the sky, it is I." "I can beat you," boasted Raven. So the two birds took off in a race for the sun. Now, in those days Raven was white and Eagle had a long straight beak of which he was very proud. All the other birds watched as Eagle and Raven flew toward the sun.

Higher and higher they flew until they were just tiny dots against the firey sun. Soon, the other birds couldn't see them any more. Raven's wings were getting very tired and he was feeling very hot as he watched Eagle fly ahead of

him toward the Sun. Suddenly, Raven saw Eagle turn away from the sun and plunge back to the earth. As Eagle flew by, Raven heard strange muttering noises but could not understand a word he was saying because the heat of the sun had melted Eagle's beak. It now curved down like a hook!

Raven laughed at the sight and kept flying toward the sun. The heat was now so powerful that he could hardly stand it but the lure of that shiny ball was so strong that Raven forced himself to fly on. Soon all Raven could see was the Sun in his face. The heat was so great that it hurt more painfully than any other hurt he had ever felt before. Finally, Raven got close enough that he could try to grab the shiny red ball of the sun. He opened his beak and clamped down hard on the Sun but he found that he could only get hold of a little bit. Still, that was better than nothing and, holding the piece of the Sun's fire in his beak, Raven triumphantly flew back to earth. Having brought fire to the earth, Raven flew proudly over the land to show the world how clever he was. He flew over a small lake whose bright shiny surface caught his eye. As he flew close to the lake he could see himself mirrored in the still waters. Raven almost fell out of the air he was so startled — his beautiful white feathers had turned to black!

Paul listened raptly as the storyteller told the children she would now tell them a story form the Haida people about how Raven is responsible for bringing the first people.

A long, long time ago there were no people in this land, only birds and animals and fish. In those days Raven travelled all over the earth. As he passed over the waves of the sea near Haida-gwai, his eye was drawn to something shiny being tossed about by the waves. He flew lower to see what it was. As he came closer, he saw a clam bobbing in the stormy seas. Raven thought he heard a noise coming from the shell, so he went nearer to find out what it was. Raven picked up the shell in his beak and carried it to the land. There he opened it and found many people. The people left the shell and were the first people of this land.

After this story was done, the teacher told her class that it was time to go home. Paul asked, "Couldn't we hear just one more story? Please?" His classmates agreed: "Yes, please tell us some more stories." The story teller laughed, and said she would, but they would have to be short as she was nearly 85 years old. She would tell them one more story that her own people, the Bella Coola, told about Raven.

We owe a lot to Raven; he brought Salmon to the people. Now Raven wanted a wife, so he and his sisters used their sharp beaks to make holes in the canoes of the salmon so they would not be able to follow them. Raven saw the beautiful daughter of the salmon chief. He asked her to help him load food into his canoe. When she stepped into Raven's canoe, he and his sisters seized her and carried her away. That's how Salmon came to Bella Coola.

Paul asked the story teller how old the stories were. She laughed and answered by asking him how long he had been in Bella Coola. Paul stammered that he had only lived here for a month. "These stories," she told him, "are as old as the people. We've been here for thousands of years since the beginning of time in this place. That's how old the stories are."
What is the purpose of such stories as these? Do some research to find out about other creation stories or stories that explain the origin of anaimals.

Paul Menard and his dad were out trolling for salmon on North Bentick Arm, about eight kilomtetres from Bella Coola, British Columbia. The late-afternoon sun sat on the tops of the hills, casting long shadows over the cool salt water. Paul sat in the bow watching the tall cedars and Douglas firs drift by. Their boat was travelling slowly, and Paul had lots of time to think as he waited for the fish to bite.

He looked back along Bentick Arm toward Bella Coola. The long arm of the sea made Paul curious. It looked like a deep trench cut between the mountains. "Dad," he asked, "was Bentick Arm once a valley? It sure looks like a valley that's been flooded bt the sea."

"Yes," replied his father, "Bentick Arm is what they call a *fjord*. That's a norwegian word. The west coast of Norway is made up of hundreds of fjords. When we get home we'll look up in the encyclopaedia and find out how fjords are made."

1. Find Bella Coola in your atlas.
2. How far is it from Vancouver to Bella Coola? From your community?
3. How would you get to Bella Coola? Look at your map again. Can you think of at least three ways you might travel to Bella Coola from Vancouver?

Did You Know?

A fjord is a glacial valley that has been invaded by the sea?

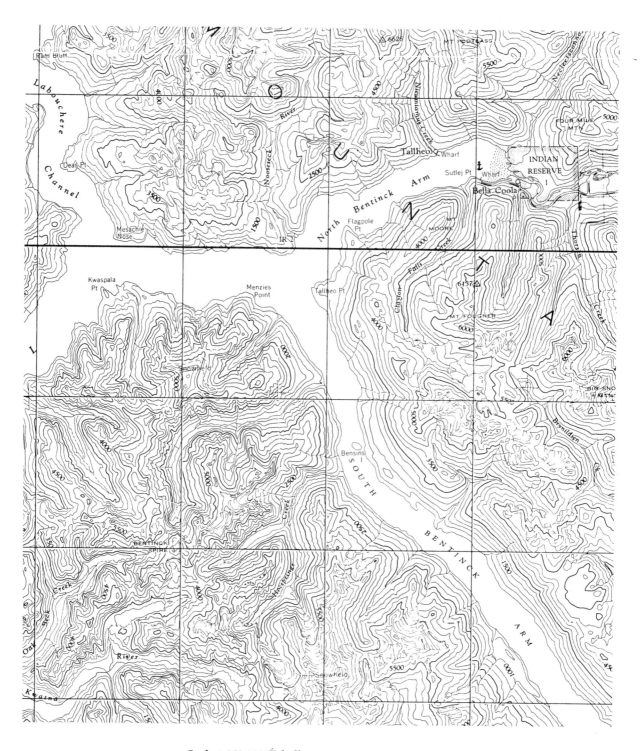

Scale 1:250,000 Échelle

Miles 5   0   5 Milles

Kilometres 5   0   5 Kilomètres

BELLA COOLA
93D
EDITION 1

A Topographic Map

1. Look up the word *topographic* in your dictionary. List the kinds of things that are shown on topographic maps. How are they different from other kinds of maps? Find other examples of topographic maps.

2. Find Bella Coola on the map.

3. What is the highest point on the map? Can you tell for sure?

4. What is the lowest point? How do you know for sure?

5. According to the map, where do the Indian people live?

Drawing a Cross Section

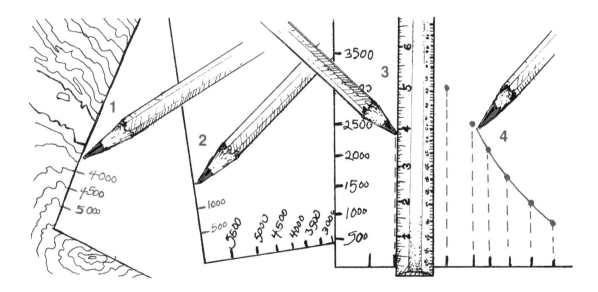

1. To draw a cross section of Bentick Arm from Mt. Pootlass lay a piece of graph paper on the map with the bottom edge touching these two places. Where each contour line touches the paper put a pencil mark and write the elevation.

2. When all the contour lines have been marked across the bottom, write the elevations up the side of the paper, from lowest to highest, at regular intervals.

3. Using a ruler, draw a dotted line up from each mark at the bottom of the paper until it is even with the same number on the graph (i.e. the 2500-foot line comes up to the 2500-foot level on the graph) and draw a dot.

4. Join all the dots. Pretend you are standing on the wharf at Tallheo. Describe what you would probably see as you look around. How does the cross section help you with this?

What is the climate like

1. Here are three climographs. Use an atlas to find where these places are and locate them on the map on pages 12-13. Where are they in relation to Bella Coola?
2. What would the average temperature be for each place in July? What would it be in January? What pattern do you see?
3. How much rainfall would you expect during an average summer (June, July, August) at each place? What would the rainfall be during the winter? What pattern do you see?
4. Here are three more climographs. Find these places in your atlas. Compare their locations with Vancouver, Prince Rupert, and Juneau.
5. What patterns do you see in these climographs? Compare them with the first three climographs.
6. The climate figures for Vancouver, Prince Rupert, and Juneau were measured near sea level. Why is it important to know this?

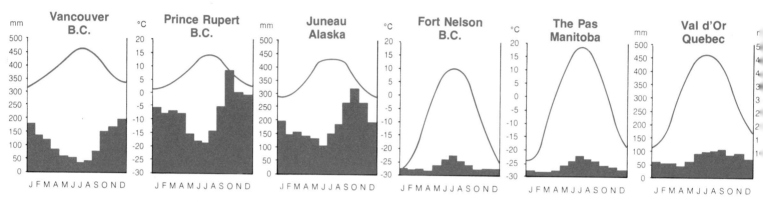

Marine Coast Climates

The climate of the Northwest Coast is known as a marine climate. The diagram shows what happens in a typical area with this kind of climate.

1. Tell what is happening at each of the letters on the diagram and explain why it is occurring. Ask your science teacher for help if you are uncertain.
2. How does the diagram explain how fjords are formed?
3. There are still glaciers in the mountains along the Northwest Coast, but far fewer than when the fjords were being formed. What causes glaciers to retreat?
4. Could the glaciers start to grow again? What would cause this?

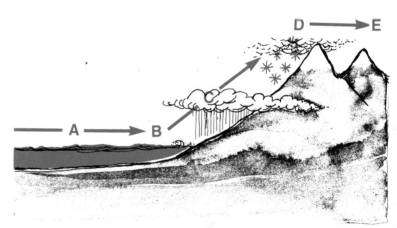

THE OLD VILLAGE

As they headed back to town, Paul caught sight of something half hidden among the giant trees — some sort of carved animal, all cracked and bleached by the wind and rain.

"Hey, let's go look," he shouted to his father.

Even before they nudged against the bank, Paul jumped out and ran up the slope. It was a pole, made from a tree trunk and carved with designs. Other poles lay rotting on the ground, and there was a pile of logs and boards, as though some sort of building had fallen down.

"What was it?" asked Paul.

"Just an old Indian village," replied his father. "The Indians all moved away years ago."

Paul was fascinated as he wandered among the rotting boards and poles, now nearly covered with underbrush. In his imagination he could picture Indian chiefs and princesses, canoes, totem poles — a whole lost village. He would have spent the rest of the day there if his father hadn't dragged him away.

Paul spent the whole of the trip back to Bella Coola wondering about the people who had lived in that old village. Who were they? Where did they come from? What did their houses look like? How many people lived there? What kind of clothes did they wear? What did they eat?

He kept asking questions his father couldn't answer. Finally his father threw up his hands. "OK, OK," he laughed, "I give up. The person you should talk to is Rose Sailor — she's a member of the Bella Coola Indian band and she knows about how they lived in the old days. She's a teacher in the school. I work with Tom Sailor at the mill and he said she's preparing a big display on Bella Coola Indian life right now."

The Bulletin Board

The next day, Paul rode his bicycle through the rain to the school. As he entered the library he saw that the walls were covered with masks, blankets, and Indian carvings. In one corner, a young, dark-haired woman was putting a photograph up on the bulletin board.

Paul had been fascinated by the story teller who had come to the school the day before. Now, he was looking for more information about the Bella Coola and other original peoples of the Pacific Coast.

"Well, here's something you can start with,' she continued, leading him over to the corkboard. "These pictures were taken in and around Bella Coola nearly a hundred years ago. The village you saw was probably abandoned even then."

"Did the old villages look like these?"

"Yes, but the pictures also show a lot of outside influences. The Bella Coola had been in contact with Europeans for many years when those pictures were taken," she answered. "If you want to find out what life was like in the village you saw you'll have to look to other sources as well."

1. Do you think the Sailors have a traditional Bella Coola name? How might Ms. Sailor's great-grandfather have received his name?
2. Look at the photographs and make a list of things that are of Bella Coola Indian origin. Which things that you can see were introduced by the Europeans?

BELLA COOLA & REGION ABOUT 100 YEARS AGO

Lame Charlie

Talleo Village

3. Have any been put together to make some thing that is neither European nor traditional Bella Coola?

4. Look closely at the house pole. What do you think it shows? Why do you think it was carved that way?

5. Did Lame Charlie's clothing come from Bella Coola? Why is he wearing a chain across his vest?

6. Examine the picture of the ocean-going canoe. It is an old Indian design; however, something of Europen origin has been added. What is it?

Ocean-going Canoe

Mask of Qomoqua

Kimsquit Village

Indian canoes pass *HMS Boxer* at anchor in Friendly Cove, 1874

Paul wanted to know if the Bella Coola were the only Indian people who lived in the area. Mrs. Sailor replied, "the Bella Coola were the only Indian people in this particular area. Our nearest neighbours were the Bella Bella who live on the islands near the mouth of Dean Channel. But the Bella Coola and the Bella Bella were only two of many groups of Indian peoples living along the west coast of North America before the white man came."

In addition to the Bella Coola the other main groups that lived along the Northwest coast were the Tlingit, Haida, Tsimshian, Kwakiutl, Nootka, Slaish, and Chinook.

These were not "tribes" in the way we usually think of a tribe. These names are used for groups of tribes and sub-tribes that all spoke the same language. Each of these was divided even further into villages, which were all separate and independent.

The Bella Bella, for example, were one of many tribes that made up the Kwakiuti group.

The Tsimshian were divided into three major tribes — the Coast Tsimshian, the Niska (who lived on the Nass River), and the Gitksan (who lived on the Skeena)

Despite the fact that they spoke different languages, these groups shared a common way of life or *culture*, known as the Northwest Coast Indian culture. This culture was found from Oregon to Alaska, and it was very different from all other Indian cultures.

1. What does the word *culture* mean to you? Write down a definition using your own words.

2. Compare your definition with those of other people in the class. How many different meanings can you come up with? Can you work out a definition that satisfies everyone?

3. Look up *culture* in a dictionary. How many meanings are given? Which was the closest to the one you decided on?

4. How could the Indians of the Northwest Coast all belong to the same culture if they spoke different languages?

5. What culture do you belong to?

Before Europeans came to the area, most Northwest Coast Indians lived in a narrow strand along the coast between the Strait of Juan de Fuca and Yakutat Bay in southern Alaska. When the first Spanish sailing ships arrived there were perhaps 75,000 to 100,000 Northwest Coast Indians — certainly no more than 150,000.

1. Find the Strait of Juan de Fuca and Yakutat Bay in your atlas. Locate them on the map.
2. Which of the groups on the map lived between the Strait of Juan de Fuca and Yakutat Bay? Do any of them still live there? Where could you find out?
3. Is 100,000 people a large population? Make a list of towns in Canada with a population of more than 100,000.
4. From what you have read so far, tell what you think life would have been like for the Indians of the Pacific Northwest.
5. What type of houses do you think they would build? Make a sketch. What sorts of things might you expect to see in their art? How do you think a person's wealth might have been measured?
6. How would this life have been different from that of other North American Indians? List as many differences as you can think of.
7. Europeans did not come to the Northwest Coast until quite recently (compared to other parts of North America). What do you think kept them away?
8. Find out how people live in this area today.

Did You Know

Not all the Northwest Coast people lived along the fjords. Some lived many kilometres inland along the rivers.

1. Suggest reasons why some villages were built along the sea while others were built along rivers.
2. Do you think that life in a river-side village would be very different from life in a seacoast village? How?

"Not all the Indians of the Northwest Coast lived exactly the same way," explained Rose. "There were differences in language, in social customs, in diet, and in art. However, there were many important things that were shared by all the Northwest Coast Indians but not by any other peoples, and that's what we mean by a culture."

The Northwest Coast culture included:

1. use of wood instead of stone or other raw materials
2. eating of fish and other seafoods as the basis of their diet
3. a distinctive style of art
4. a person's importance or status in the community based on wealth
5. religions that included worship of animals and supernatural spirits
6. village life in large, permanent houses, usually at good fishing spots
7. a distinctive style of clothes

How Do We Know?

"Mrs. Sailor," asked Paul, "how do we know what it was like long ago? Nobody lives that way any more. The Indians didn't have writing, so they couldn't have records of what it was like."

"There are several kinds of evidence about life in the old days," replied Rose. "Many artifacts have survived — things like bowls, dishes, canoes, masks, tools, and the totem poles that most people are familiar with. Some of the white men who visited the area in the very early days wrote descriptions of what they saw, or drew pictures. The photos you saw show European influences but they still tell a lot about the Indian culture. More recently scientists called anthropologists set out to record the songs, stories, legends and customs of the Indians before too much was lost or forgotten. And even when people have moved away and their villages have almost disappeared; we can still tell a lot about how they lived by digging up the village sites and looking at what is left. The people who do this are called archeologists, and you'd be amazed at what they can find out."

1. What is evidence? How is it different from ordinary things? What is an artifact? How are artifacts; different from ordinary things?
2. Look up anthropologist in your dictionary. Find out what anthropologists do, and how they go about their work. Look up archeology, and find out how archeologists work. How are they like anthropologists? How are they different?

"The most important thing to remember, though," continued Rose, "is that ours is still a living culture. A lot of things have changed or disappeared, but Indian parents still pass on stories about the old ways to their children. And just because we didn't write things on paper doesn't mean we have no records. For example, the carvings on totem poles are ways of recording things. If you know how to read them they can give you important clues, not only about how the Indians lived, but about what they thought and believed. Here's a Gitksan story from the old days. Look at the picture and see if you can pick out the pole that goes with the story."

How Tewalsu's Family Got the Dog-Salmon Crest

A young man of the Tewalsu family once showed great respect to some salmon his relatives had dried. By doing this, he cured the Chief of the Salmon of a terrible sickness. The salmon, happy that their chief was well, came to his house disguised as human beings. They met him with a dugout canoe at the river's edge. Then they took him to their home at the mouth of the river.

There the salmon tribe lived in three huge houses. On the front of one was painted the dog salmon. On the front of the second was the steelhead salmon.

Group of totem poles at the
Gitksan village of Kitwanga
on the Skeena River.

On that of the third house a spring slamon was painted. The salmon who lived in these houses acted like human beings.

When the time for the yearly salmon run came, the salmon gave the young man a salmon suit. When he put it on he changed into a salmon. He swam upstream with a school of salmon until he reached the canyon where his village was located.

There his uncle Raraotsren was fishing. Raraotsren caught a salmon so huge he could hardly drag it out of the water. Inside its body, he discovered his nephew — still alive! The dog salmon became the family crest and the family enjoyed great status and importance in the village.

1. What does this story suggest about the importance of salmon to the Northwest Coast Indians?
2. According to the story, what sort of ideas and beliefs did the Indian have about salmon? How do you think they might have got these ideas? What do they suggest about the culture of the Northwest Coast Indians?
3. Why do you think the dog salmon crest was so important to the Tewalsu family? How did they show off their family crest? What does this suggest about their culture?
4. A totem is a sort of crest or badge. It is a symbol that belongs to a particular person or group of people. Make a list of crests or badges that are used by members of your class. Are any of them like an Indian totem? In what way? What do they tell you about your way of life?
5. Try to list six other things that the story suggests about the Northwest Coast Indian culture. Can you be sure about your ideas? How could you check them?
6. Why is it important to use several sources of information to get an accurate idea of a culture?

NORTHWEST COAST INDIAN COMMUNITIES

Most of the Northwest Coast Indian people lived in village communities. Some of these villages were very large, with several hundred people. Others had only a few houses.

1. Look at the pictures of the villages. What do they have in common? How do they differ? Do you think that Northwest Coast Indian villages looked like before Europeans arrived? How might they have been different? Make a list of signs of European contact you can see in the pictures.

Examine the houses closely. Can you tell what they are made of? How could you check your answer? How big are they? Are they bigger or smaller than houses in your community?

2. Name two ways in which the Northwest Coast Indian houses are similar to houses in your Community. Name two ways in which they are different?

3. Can you tell from the photographs how many rooms these houses might have? Estimate the number of rooms. How many people might live in each house? In each village?

Village on the Salmon River.

The Kwakiuti village of Nahwitti, around 1880

"We know what Bella Coola houses and villages were like before the Europeans came," said Rose. "The explorer Alexander Mackenzie, the first white person to reach the Pacific by land, travelled down the Bella Coola River in 1793. He wrote about a Bella Coola village in his diary:"

Mackenzie's Journal — July 1793

I then made a tour of the village. There were four houses built on raised platforms made of logs and seven built right on the ground. Beside the houses, there were other buildings. These were used as kitchens or to smoke fish. The houses are made by placing several log posts into the earth. On top of these logs other logs and planks are placed to make a floor. The floor is four metres above the ground.

The buildings are 30 to 40 metres long and about 12 metres wide. Along the centre of the house are four or five fireplaces. These are used both for warmth and for the smoking of fish. Walls of cedar divide the building into apartments about two metres by two metres. Boards resting on beams running across the house form their beds. On these planks they also place cedar boxes that hold food, tools, and thier other possessions. Roasted fish hang from poles that run along the roof beams of the house. The whole building is well covered with planks and bark — except for a few centimetres along the ridgepole. This opening lets the smoke out and allows some light to enter the house. The houses that rest on the ground are built of the same material. They are built to the same plan as the raised houses.

1. Why do you think some of the Bella Coola houses were built on raised platforms while others were built on the ground?
2. Why do you think the Bella Coola houses were so big? Can you figure out how many apartments there were in a Bella Coola house? How many people do you think lived in the houses Mackenzie saw? Would they all be members of the same family?
3. Draw a picture of what you think the inside of the Bella Coola house might have looked like.

Mackezie's Journal

When we were surrounded by the natives on our arrival, I counted some 65 men. Some of the men may have been away from the village. I calculate the population of this village to be at least 200 souls.

Near the chief's house I saw several large panels of wood — about seven metres by three metres in size. They were made of thick cedar boards, joined so neatly they looked like one piece of wood. They were painted with hieroglyphics and pictures of many different animals. They were done with a degree of skill I had not expected in such primitive people.

I did not learn what they were used for.

They appeared to be used in religious festivals performed twice a year in the spring and summer.

There was a large building in the centre of the village that I thought was an unfinished house. It was about 18 metres by 15, each end of which was marked by stout poles set in the ground. The corner posts were plain, about three metres high. The two centre poles at each end were nearly a metre across and carved in the shape of human beings. They were four metres high and support the ridge poles on their heads. The poles, posts, and figures were painted red and black. The sculptures of these people is superior to their painting.

A Bella Coola house front around 1880.

1. Compare Mackenzie's description of the Bella Coola house with the photograph.
2. Find out what hieroglyphics are. Did Mackenzie really find hieroglyphics at Bella Coola?
3. What does Mackenzie's journal tell us about European attitudes toward Indian art and culture?
4. Why, do you suppose, did the Bella Coola have special religious celebrations in the spring and summer? Look at the names of the months in the Bella Coola calendar on page 30.

Several families, usually related to each other, lived together; a chief would have a very large house in which ten or more families might live. Each family had its own room or special area against one of the walls. At the centre of the house was an open area with cooking fires for the various families and a large fire at the very centre for heat. People were always coming and going. Food was shared. Anyone who was in the house would receive some.

Inside a Coast Salish house as painted by Paul Kane around 1845.

Inside a house at Nootka Sound, as drawn by John Webber, an artist who visited the Northwest Coast with Captain Cook 1778.

1. Look at the painting of the Salish house and estimate how big it is. How does it compare with Mackenzie's estimate of the Bella Coola houses? Is it designed and built in the same way?

2. Look at the pictures of the Nootka house. What kind of floor does this house have? How does it differ from the Bella Coola house described by Mackenzie?

3. What is hanging from the roof beams of the Nootka house? Why are they there?

4. Write a story about what it would have been like to live in a Northwest Coast Indian house. Look at what you have written. Would it be different if it had been written by someone who had never seen electric lights, furnaces, or windows?

BUILDING A HOUSE

"How did the indians ever raise those heavy house posts and lift the beams into place?" asked Paul. "Did they have pulleys or cranes?" "No," repied Mrs. Sailor, "I'll draw pictures to show you how they did it. Can you figure it out?"

1. Look at the picture of the house post being erected. Why did the Indians put the log under it? How were the beams raised to the top of the posts? What do we call this way of lifting or moving something?

2. The Indians had no nails. Can you tell how the houses were held together? How were the planks and logs cut? What kinds of tools do you think were used?

3. Make models showing how the Northwest Coast Indians built their houses. Try to show the different stages of construction.

Building a house at Gwayasdums village, 1900

House pots were sometimes beautifully carved, as in this Koskimo house.

House frame at Memkumlis village.

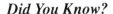

Did You Know?

Although the Northwest Coast Indians lived in permanent villages some groups also built temporary summer villages at important fishing spots along a river. These were often just temporary camps, but some groups built wooden houses like their winter homes. The Nootka, for example, built house frames at both their summer and winter sites. When they moved from one to the other they took down the roofs and walls, loaded the planks into their canoes, and put them up on the other frames.

1. What does the Salish summer camp building in the picture below appear to be made of?
2. Suggest reasons why the Salish might have made temporary summer villlages.
3. Why have winter villages?
   Why not build the permanent village at the summer fishing spots?

Wood was one of the most important natural resources to the Indians of the Northwest Coast. Like the other peoples of the area, the Bella Coola were master carpenters and carvers. They made most of their tools and other household goods from wood. The most important wood was red cedar, which grew in large numbers everywhere. From cedar they made everything from giant house poles to small dishes. Other trees such as spruce, hemlock, and Douglas fir were more common, but were not used because they were harder to work. Cedar was just about perfect for woodworking. The trees grew tall and straight, with a fine, even grain for splitting. The wood was soft enough to carve easily, and it did not decay quickly in the moist climate.

How Planks Were Made

Houses, smoke houses, boardwalks, and ceremonial screens were made of planks. A tall cedar tree, straight and free of knots, was felled, and the bark stripped away. Wedges, made of wood hardened in a fire, were driven into the log along the grain, and the planks split off. The planks were then shaped and finished using an adze.

Cooking boxes and other watertight containers were also made from cedar planks. Boxes were used for carrying water, holding fish and other foods, and even for cooking.

Making a cedar box

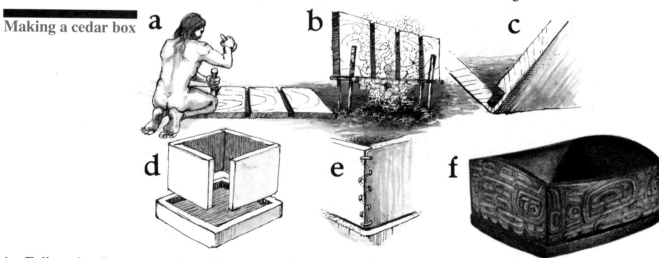

1. Follow the diagrams and see if you can tell what is happening at each step. How would you make sure the box is watertight?
2. What is an adze? How is it used? What tools would we use nowadays instead of an adze?
3. The most common way of cooking fish was to boil it. How did the Bella Coola do this without burning the wooden cooking box?

Dishes and serving bowls were also made of cedar. Ordinary dishes were plain, but some, like this Haida bowl, were beautifully carved and were used on special occasions.

During ceremonies such as the potlatch, giant feast dishes were used to serve the guests.

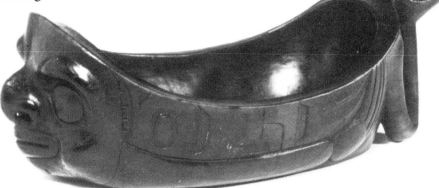

1. How big do you think the feast dish is? How much food would it hold?

CANOES

The Norhtwest Coast peole built two main types of canoes. One was used for travelling on rivers, the other for the open sea. River canoes were up to ten metres long and might carry up to four persons. They were usually poled. Paddles were used in deep water. The seagoing canoes were longer, usually around fifteen metres in length, and might carry up to ten passengers. The Haida and Nootka built enormous seagoing canoes that could carry forty people and travel far out of sight of land.

1. Can you follow the steps in the pictures below? Why do you think the canoe-builder started by cutting a small hole into the base of the tree? Tell what is happening in the other pictures.

Making a Canoe

24

1. Seagoing canoes were long, tall and narrow. The river canoes were shorter, lower, and wider. Can you suggest any reasons for the difference in design?
2. Bella Coola canoes were usually black with fish designs painted in white. Many West Coast Indians painted fish designs on thier canoes. Suggest some reasons for this.

Mrs. Sailor showed Paul a stone that looked like an axe head. "It's a stone grinder," she explained. "One of the old men once showed me how grinders were used with sand to smooth the wood before the canoe was painted."

"Many Northwest Coast Indians also used a kind of "sandpaper" made of the dried skin of the dogfish shark to give a smooth finish to things made of wood."

3. Find out why the skin of the dogfish can be used as sandpaper. Is the dogfish a real fish?
4. How do we smooth wood today? Can you find any ways that we smooth wood that are similar to the ways the West Coast Indians used?
5. Carve a model of a dug-out canoe.
6. Make a full-sized picture of a Bella Coola river canoe and a seagoing canoe. Decorate them and hang them on the wall. Are they bigger than you thought they would be?

Did You Know?

The Indians kept on using their canoes even after seeing European ships, but they made one change — they added a sail. The canoes, however, did not have a keel or a rudder and could only sail with the wind, not across it or against it.

BARK AND ROOTS

Cedar bark, too, was used for many things by peoples of the Northwest Coast. The women would soak the bark and pound it with a stone to separtate it into strips. Then they hung it over a wooden frame or a canoe paddle and beat it again until it was soft enough to bend. The soft bark was woven into blankets, skirts, and raincapes, or braided to make rope and fish nets.

Strips of cedar bark were also used to weave rain hats. Important people had hats woven from the soft roots of the spruce tree. They were used to keep the rain off, but they also showed that the person was rich and important. They were worn at special ceremonies like the potlach. They were usually painted with one of the owner's crests.

Pounding cedar bark

John Webber drew this picture of a weaver at work at Nootka Sound in 1778

1. Look closely at the woman in the picture opposite, and describe her clothes. What is she carrying in her hand? How is it used? What is she carrying on her back? How might this material be related to the tool and to her clothes?
2. The woman at the right is decorating a hat woven from spruce roots. Compare it with the cedar bark cape she is wearing.
3. The woman is wearing several pieces of jewelry. Which are similar to jewelry that women wear today? Which are different?
4. The design on the hat on the left shows a picture of a beaver. What do you think the one on the right shows? Suggest what type of animal the tail on the hat at the right came from.

Decorating a spruce root rain hat

Haida rain hats

 **FISHING**

Fish were the most important source of food to the Indians of the Northwest Coast. The people were expert fishermen who used as many different ways of catching fish as there were fish to catch — nets, spears, traps, bows, arrows, weirs, hooks, harpoons, even a type of rake to catch small fish like herring and oolachan.

1. One of these fish traps was located at, or very near, the ocean and would only work there. Which one is it? How do you know? Explain how it worked. Make a series of drawings to illustrate your description. How would you go about building it? Could you use a trap like this for all types of fish?

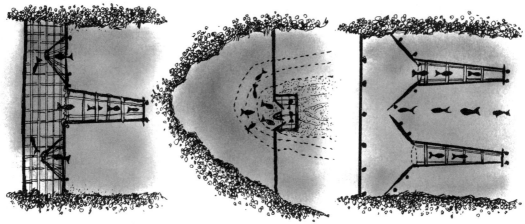

2. The other traps were designed for rivers or streams. Make a series of drawings to show how they work. One is for a small stream, the other for a large stream or river. Which is which?

3. The head of the harpoon was designed to separate from the shaft when it struck a salmon. Why was this a good design? How would the fisherman land the fish?

1. Look at the pictures on this page and name three kinds of fishing shown.
2. What are the advantages and disadvantages of each? What kind of fish would be taken by each method?
3. Do you think the bow and arrow was used much? What problems would the hunter face in using it at the seashore?

4. Nowadays, it is illegal to fish with dip nets like the Indains did. Why is this so? Does this mean that the old ways were wrong? Why not? How do people fish for salmon nowadays?

SALMON

Salmon were by far the most important fish. They were caught by the thousands during the spring and summer. The names of some of the months in the Bella Coola calendar show how important salmon was to these people.

Siisamt: Time for eating spring salmon (sixth moon after the winter solstice)

Sikatamtak: Time for sockeye salmon to come up the river (first moon after summer solstice)

Siistalitt: Time for eating dog salmon (second moon after summer solstice)

Siiswaist: Time for eating cohoe salmon (third moon after summer solstice)

Sigalxam: Time for gathering fern roots (fourth moon after summer solstice)

Siqulxwaix: Time of the gathering of supernatural beings (fifth moon after summer solstice)

Sicmt: Sun sits down (sixth moon after summer solstice)

1. In what month, by the European calendar, does the sockeye salmon arrive?
2. What is the summer solstice? On what date does it occur? The winter solstice?
3. Why do you think the Bella Coola gather fern roots?
4. What month in our calendar is the "time of the gathering of supernatural beings?" What event in our culture occurs then?
5. Why might the Bella Coola have called the sixth month after the summer soltice "Sun sits down?"

Salmon were usually caught at the mouths of rivers, at waterfalls and rapids, or where the rivers formed narrow canyons. Where the rivers narrowed, the Indians used to build huge fish traps called weirs. In 1793 the explorer Alexander Mackenzie described how the people caught salmon using a weir.

Mackenzie's journal

Salmon is very abundant in the Bella Coola River. The people have a constant and plentiful supply of this excellent fish. To catch them more easily, they have built a great weir across the river. Using the weir they can catch fish on either side of it.

I said that I would like to look at the weir but these people are very superstitious about their salmon. They would not let me get any closer than the river bank. The river is some fifty metres wide. By watching a man with a dipnet, I determined that the river is three to four metres deep.

The weir itself is a work that required much labour. It is very skillfully built. It is built out from the bank of the river 120 cm above the water. It stops about two-thirds of the river's flow. It is made of small trees stuck into the river bottom at an angle (to do so they must have built the weir when the water was very low). Over the small trees is poured a layer of gravel. Next comes a layer of smaller trees. The pattern of trees and gravel is repeated until the weir reaches its full height.

At the bottom of the weir there are nets and traps. Salmon fall into these traps as they try to leap over the weir. On each side of the weir, there is a framework of timber, two metres above the level of the water on the upstream side. In this framework there are passages that lead straight into the traps. Salmon that escape the traps are caught at the bottom of the fall with dipnets.

Did You Know?

Salmon can jump up waterfalls over a metre in height. The weirs were built just high enough that the fish could not jump over them. The same thing happens when dams are built. To let the salmon get to their spawning grounds, engineers must build fish ladders around the dams.

A Coast Salish fish weir on the Cowichan River

The Bella Coola Salmon were believed to live in five villages under the sea and look like human beings. Every spring the salmon people put on fish clothing and swam up the rivers to give food to the Indian people. When a salmon was caught, the Indians believed that it returned to its village under the sea, leaving its flesh for the people to eat. The first salmon each spring was thought to be a scout and only a chief could catch it. The chief would make a speech honouring the fish. Then it would be eaten and all its bones thrown back into the river. If this was not done, the Bella Coola believed that the rest of the salmon would not come. If the people did not show proper respect to the salmon, the scout would not return to his village to lead the rest of the salmon to the Indians.

A Coast Salish Salmon Story

Steelhead came up to the Cowlitz River first. With him were five kinds of little fish. He spawned far up the Cowlitz and then started back down to the sea. At Mossy Rock, he met Chinook Salmon. Chinook had five kinds of little fish with him. All were very thin and bony.

"How's the country up the river where you've been?" Chinook asked.

"I'm going to fix him," thought Steelhead. Out loud he said, "Oh it's very nice. There are many nice shallow pools where high-born fish can float belly-up."

Chinook got very angry. It was true that, after spawning, he would not return alive. Instead he would die and float back down the river.

"Let's kill him" Chinook cried to his friends. He jumped onto Steelhead and grabbed his fat which he put on himself. He tore off Steelhead's head and put it on himself. His own head, which was full of bones, he put on Steelhead.

Steelhead went home and came back the following year. Chinook went on up the river, spawned, then died.

Since that time, the Steelhead has had poor quality meat and a skinny back compared to the Salmon. After spawning, Chinook gets old and dies, and floats down the river belly up. Steelhead never dies; after spawning he allways goes back to the ocean to return again next year.

1. Which do you think the Coast Salish preferred — Steelhead or Chinook Salmon? Why?
2. Why do the salmon come to the rivers of the Pacific Coast each year?
3. Find out how salmon spawn. Is the story accurate about what happens?

Oolachan

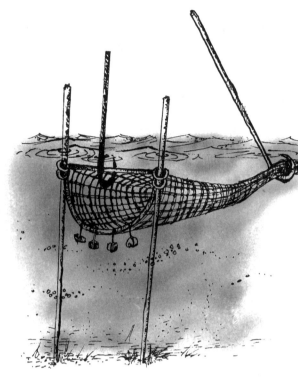

Next to salmon the oolachan was the most important fish to the Indians. The oolachan is small and looks much like a herring.

Thousands of these slow-swimming little fish entered the Bella Coola and other rivers to spawn in late April or early May. The Indians caught them in specially-designed nets which were set out in shallow, fast-running water near the mouths of the rivers.

1. The mouth of the net faces upstream, the same way the oolachan are swimming. How, then , are the fish caught? (Re-read the paragraph above for clues.)
2. How is the net emptied?
3. According to Indian tradition the oolachan net was invented by a young Kwakiutl girl some time during the eighteenth century. Where might she have got the idea?
4. Two other methods of catching oolachen are shown here. Tell how each works. What advantages and disadvantages do they have compared to the oolachan net?

Some oolachan were dried for thier meat but the most important part of the oolachen was its oil or greases. The fish were allowed to rot for two or three weeks in a pit dug in the ground. This made it easier to get the oil out and was also thought to improve the flavour. The fish were then boiled or pressed to get the oil out.

Oolachan oil could be stored in cedar boxes for a long time. It was used as a sauce or relish with other foods. Fresh berries with oolachan oil was a special treat. The Bella Coola thought it a sign of poverty if a person had to eat berries without oolachan oil!

A herring rake in action

Bella Coola oolachan trap

Oolachan drying at Fishery
Bay on the Nass River, 1884

A "mess" of oolachan
ripening in a pit

Bringing the catch to shore

Did You Know?

The biggest oolachan run on the coast took place on the Nass River. Nass grease was the best-tasting of all — even the Bella Coola agreed that it was better than theirs.

Oolachan grease was an important trade item.

The Bella Coola and other coast peoples traded with Indians in the interior who gave moose and caribou hides in exchange for the oil. The routes they followed are still known as "grease trails."

There were no oolachan streams in the islands where the Haida lived. Every year they visited the Nass to trade for oolachan grease with the Tsimshian.

Haida women cleaning the halibut catch at Neah Bay

Halibut

After Salmon, halibut was the most important staple fish for the Indians of the Northwest Coast. There were rich fishing banks near the Queen Charlotte Islands, and both the Haida and Southern Kwakiutl caught halibut there.

1. What is meant by a staple food?
2. The halibut is a large fish, and spends all its life in the ocean. Why would fishing hooks be a good way of catching halibut?
3. The Indians also used other methods for catching halibut. What might these be?
4. What differences are there between salmon fishing and halibut fishing? Explain your ideas.
5. Look at the fish hooks. Are they similar to the fish hooks we use today? What do you suppose the Indians used to make their fish hooks? Try to find out. Make a fish hook from these materials and see if you can catch a fish with it.

Fish hooks

Their baskets filled with shellfish and their seaweed, these Nootka women wait for the canoe that will take them home to the village.

Other Food From the Sea

The sea provided food other than fish. Clams, mussels and other shellfish could be dug from the mud at low tide. They were a staple food almost as important as fish. The meat of seals that swam up the fjords was considered a great delicacy. Seal served at a potlach was a great luxury indeed. Even seaweed was gathered and eaten.

Some Indians travelled many kilometres out to sea to hunt seals and other sea mammals, including whales.

1. According to the picture, about how big was the whaling harpoon?
2. What would happen to the harpoon when it struck a whale? Why is it a good design?

How the harpoon was made

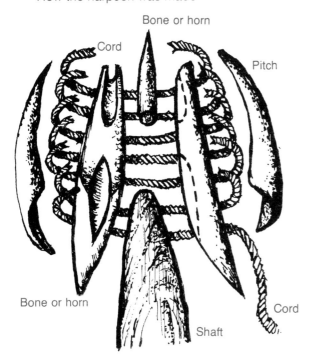

A Nootka whaler

Plan of a Nootka whaling canoe

P — Paddler
S — Steersman
H — Harpooner
F — Float

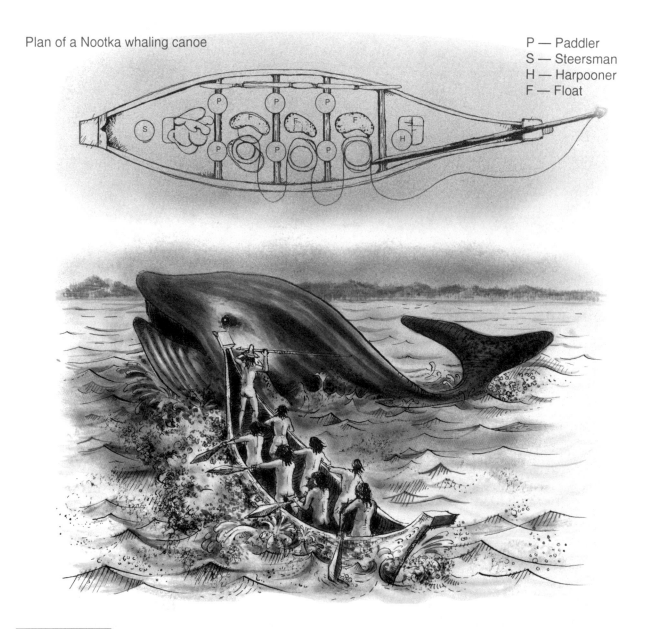

A Whale Hunt

The greatest whalers were the Nootka on Vancouver Island. only a great chief could afford to operate a whaling canoe. The whaling canoe carried a small but highly trained crew of six paddlers, a steersman, and the harpooner. The harpooner was a very important man, usually the chief of the village or a close relative.

1. The whaling crew and their canoe was always organized according to the same pattern, and a strike was alwasy made in the same way. From the drawing, and the plan of the canoe, describe what you think each man did during a whale hunt.

Did You Know?

Only the Nootka hunted whales actively, but they and other tribes such as the Haida had special rituals which, they believed, caused dead whales to drift ashore near their villages. Hunting whales by ritual was believed to be just as good as hunting by harpoon.

"Many people find it hard to understand our art," chuckled Rose, "but we don't have any trouble because we know how to recognize the different designs. In fact, all Northwest Coast Indian art is very similar. The same shapes and forms appear in carvings, paintings, and weavings.

"Look at these two designs. The one on the left is part of a Chilkat blanket. The one on the right is from a wooden panel. They look different because the carver was able to cut curves in the wood while the weaver had to work mostly in straight lines. But look closely and you'll see the patterns are the same.

"Almost every design shows an animal or a supernatural creature that was important in our religion. Each character has certain clues and you see if you can figure out which one is which."

1. Raven has a long, straight beak
2. Eagle has a heavy beak that curves down at the tip
3. Hawk's beak curves back to touch his face
4. Killer Whale has a tall fin on his back and a tail with two flukes
5. Bear has a big mouth with teeth (and his tongue sometimes sticks out)
6. Wolf is like Bear but his snout is usually longer and thinner
7. Frog has big bug-eyes and a wide mouth and thick lips

"Hey," said Paul, "that's only seven."

"Yes," laughed Rose. "I want to see if you can guess the last one yourself. But I'll give you a little help — look at his teeth, they should tell you who he is."

1. Look at the carvings on the following pages and see how many characters you can identify.
2. Find books of West Coast Indian art in the library and see how many other characters you can pick out. Make a list of the clues the artists have used to make each other distinctive.

Masks and Carving

Nearly everyone is familiar with Northwest Coast Indian art because of the famous totem poles of the area. But long before the first totem poles were carved the people of the Pacific coast were fine artists. They were best at carving, but also produced fine paintings and weavings.

These masks, carved in cedar and decorated with sea shells, copper, hair and fur, are among the finest examples of Northwest Coast Indian Art.

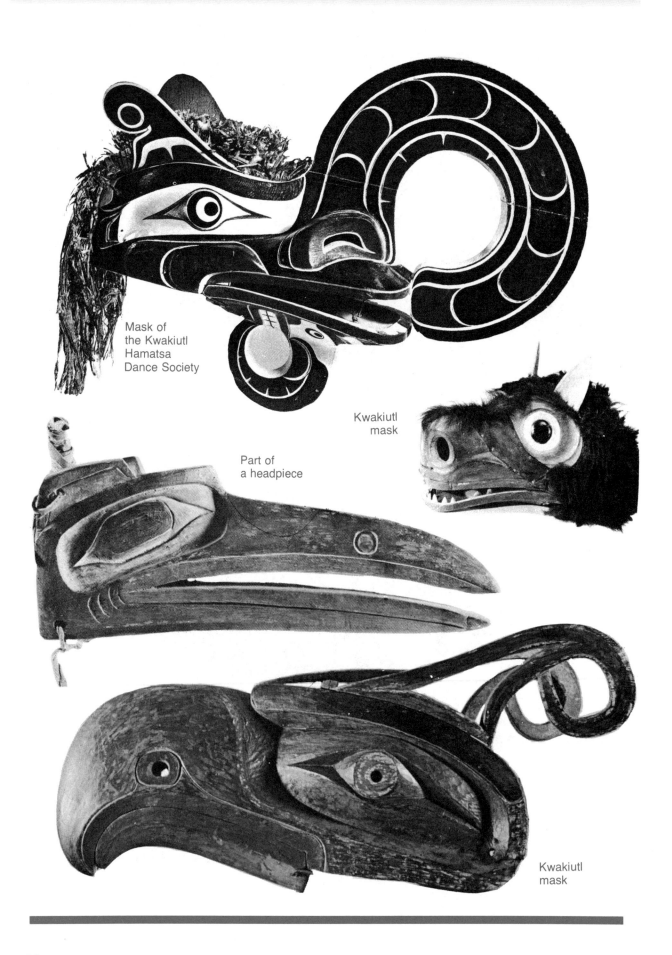

Mask of
the Kwakiutl
Hamatsa
Dance Society

Kwakiutl
mask

Part of
a headpiece

Kwakiutl
mask

Other things carved in wood were boxes, rattles, dishes, chests, clubs, canoes and paddles, to name just a few.

Tlingit chief's rattle

Kwakiutl shaman's chest

Haida bowl

Haida paddle

Haida food dish

In addition to wood, the Indians of the Northwest carved mountain goat and mountain sheep horns, bone, ivory from teeth and tusks, and occasionally stone. But wood was by far the most important material.

Stone mortar for grinding tobacco

Haida charm carved from bone

Haida artists carved slate figures like this for sale to tourists during the nineteenth century

A spoon made of horn

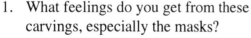

1. What feelings do you get from these carvings, especially the masks?
2. *Realistic, stylized,* and *abstract* are words that people use to describe different kinds of art. What do you think each one means? Look them up in your dictionary to check; you might also talk about them with your art teacher.
3. Which word best describes the art of the Northwest Coast people? Why?

4. Most Northwest Coast Indian art portrays animals that were of great importance to their religion. List the animals you can see here and find out the importance of these animals to the Indians.
5. Masks were used by shamans and spirit dancers in religious ceremonies. Find out about the spirit world of the Northwest Coast people, and their religious beliefs.

WEAVING AND BLANKETS

Among the Indians of the Northwest Coast carving was done only by the men. The women specialized in weaving beautiful blankets and robes. They got their wool from the mountain goat, as they had no domesticated sheep. The only domestic animal the Bella Coola had was the dog. Dog hair was also used in weaving and provided a dark contrast to the lighter goat's wool.

The most famous of coast Indian weaving styles is the Chilkat blanket. These were usually woven from mountain goat wool, but plants and dog hair were also used. These spectacular robes were woven only by the women of the Chilkut tribe of the Tlingit. They were traded far up and down the coast but they were so expensive that only great chiefs could afford them. The wool from three mountain goats was needed for one Chilkat blanket.

Chilkat blankets were made in an unusual way. First, the design was drawn on a pattern board. The weaver copied this, weaving different parts of the design separately. Then the different pieces were sewn together to make a complete blanket.

1. The blanket has two side panels, while the pattern board has only one.
   Can you explain?
2. Comment on the "loom" the weaver is using.

Among the Coast Salish, blankets were woven on a loom like the one shown in the painting by Paul Kane. The artists had very few dyes before the Europeans came. The only colours they had were yellow, black, red, and the white of the natural wool.

How the Coast Salish Made Dyes

Salish Name	Colour	How it was made
S'kayq	black	Boiling of hemlock bark or birch bark in mud containing iron Boiling fern roots in water
Skwiy	yellow	Put yellow lichen in water and bring to a boil
Sh'kwaym	Red	Twigs and bark of the red alder are boiled in a wooden vessel

The dyeing was done by placing the wool in the dye solution after the colour had been released. To keep the colours from fading a *mordant* was used. The most common mordant among the coastal Indians was urine. Until modern times urine was used all over the world as a mordant. Yellow lichen dyes did not require a mordant.

1. Look closely at the painting by Paul Kane of a Salish weaver. This type of loom is known as a two-bar loom. See if you can find out how it works. Make a model of the loom and try to weave on it.

2. Try to make some dyes from natural materials like the Salish did.
   If the materials they used are not available where you live, you can use some of the following.
   Brown - hemlock bark boiled in an enamel pot - alum mordant
   Pink - wild cherry leaves, twigs, and flowers, boiled in an enamel pot - alum mordant
   Blue - log wood (available in hobby shops or chemistry sets) boiled one hour - alum mordant
   Purple - logwood boiled one half hour - alum mordant
   You can also try various mosses and lichens or berries that grow near where you live.

THE IMPORTANCE OF WEALTH

The Indians of the Northwest measured a person's importance in the community by his wealth. Before the Europeans arrived there was no money as we know it. Wealth was counted in two ways — *goods and honours.* Goods or property were things like blankets, cedar boxes,oolachen oil, canoes, slaves — things you could touch and hold. Thses also included real property like a house, a good fishing spot, or berry picking grounds.

The other form of wealth was very different. *Honours* took the form of names, songs, crests, dances, or special rights and privileges. You could not see or feel these things except in the form of masks, totems, or other *symbols* that showed hoow important a person was. Every person in a West Coast Indian community (except slaves) had the right to use certain ceremonial names and to wear certain crests. The more honours a person owned, the more important and respected he was.

A chief who won a battle, or a person who performed a special feat of bravery, might be given a new name that celebrated the deed. However, almost all honours were inherited. Some families were rich and powerful because they owned many crests or names, and could pass these honours to their children. Other families owned very few honours and were not so rich and powerful.

Everyone in a Northwest Coast village (except the slaves) owned some riches and honours, but it was the heads of the families who had the really important names and crests and who owned the important things like houses, fishing grounds, masks and rattles. These were the chiefs of the villiage, and the head of the richest and most important family was the main chief for the whole village.

1. What does the wealth and property of the Northwest Coast Indian people tell us about their culture?:

2. From what you have read and studied, did any other native people in North America have the same ideas about property and status? What kinds of property did they have? Who owned the tribe's hunting and fishing grounds? How did they measure a person's importance?

3. How do we measure wealth in our society? Do we have any forms of wealth that cannot be measured in terms of money?

4. Do we give honours? If so, what forms do they take?

5. Do we have symbols in our society? What do they show?

6. Are the most important people in your community the wealthiest? Are we different from the Northwest Coast Indians in the ways we measure a person's importance?

"That's not fair!" burst out Paul. "A few chiefs owned everything and the rest of the people owned nothing. They didn't even have houses of their own, or places to fish."

"It looks that way at first," said Rose, "but it wasn't like that at all. Tell me, who owns the house you live in?"

"Mom and Dad do."

"But you get to live there, don't you? Well, it was like that with the West Coast Indians. The chief owned the house, but all the members of the family had a right to share it. It was the same with his honours. They belonged to the chief but all the members of the family shared the power and prestige of being part of the family. In fact they were proud of having a rich, powerful leader, and they worked to help him.

"Here's a story about a man who has just become a chief. Listen carefully and see what it tells you about the Indians of the West Coast."

Kamaxwa's Potlach

Kamaxwa, chief of the Kimnish family, was proud and happy as he watched the guests who had come to attend his potlach. Dressed in his finest robes, he stood in the place of honour at the rear of the great wooden house, the other members of the Kimnish family gathered around according to their importance.

The flames burned brightly in the fire places.

The flickering light danced on the carved house posts, the newly-painted ceremonial screen, he giant feast dishes brimming with fish and oil, and the great piles of gifts that Kamaxwa would give away to thank the guests for coming.

The ushers were showing the guests to their places along the sides of the house, each according to his proper rank. Never had so many great chiefs attende a potlach. From up and down coast they had come, some making journeys of more than a week. The house of the Kimnish was the biggest in the village, yet even it could hardly hold everyone, for behind each chief were the lesser members of his family, each acccording to his rank.

It was almost two years since the old chief, his father, had died but Kamaxwa had waited. He and his people had worked hard, hunting, fishing, weaving, carving. The spirits had been kind. Never had the Kimnish had better fortune or built up greater stores of food, oolachen oil, canoes, boxes, rattles, crests, sea otter robes, mountain goat wool and other riches — even a piece of copper from far up the coast.

Now he was ready. He would take up the title of chief, claim his crests and other honours, and adopt his proper, ceremonial name.

The last guest was seated. A hush fell over the crowded house and all eyes turned toward Kamaxwa. He waited a moment then stepped forward to begin his speech of welcome.

The potlach was about to begin!

1. At a potlach the most important guest is always seated first, in the best position. The least important is seated last, in the poorest position. Seventeen chiefs have come to Kamaxwa's potlach. Work out a seating plan for them. Tell how you did it.
2. You are Tsintax, chief of the village of Linkwistix. You are the most important guest at the potlach but you have been shown to the third most important seat. This is an insult. What will you do?
3. You are the yongest brother of Kamaxwa and have worked hard to help make the potlach a success. Describe your feelings as Kamaxwa begins his speech to the guests.

Potlaches were usually given to announce important events in a person's life. This is Kamaxwa's third. His first was given by his parents to announce that he had been born. His second came when he married.

The details of the potlach varied from place to place but the basic pattern was always the same. As host, Kamaxwa starts by

welcoming the guests and thanking them for coming. He will explain that he intends to become chief of the Kimnish family, and that he is going to adopt his ceremonial name and the crests of the family.

These are very important honours, so Kamaxwa will go over each one carefully. He will tell the history of his family back to the days of the very first men and women on earth. He will explain that his name has come down from these ancestors, and he will tell why it is such an important and powerful one. He will tell the story of each crest, and how the family came to own it. This may go on for several days and there will be feasts, songs, dances and chants to entertain the guests ands illustrate the legends.

When the potlatch is about to end, Kamaxa will give out the presents. The most important chief gets the most expensive gift, and receives it first; the least important gets the least expensive, and receives it last. These gifts are important in two ways. They thank the guests for coming, but they also help prove that Kamaxa is worthy of the honours that he has adopted. It would not be proper for a poor person to claim important honours. Only a rich person is worthy of them, and he must prove this by having a big potlach and giving away large amounts of wealth.

The guests are very impressed. No one has ever seen such rich gifts before. When they return to their villages there will be no doubt that Kamaxa is worthy of the great honours he has claimed, and people will know his name all up and down the coast.

1. Who gave you your name? How did they decide what it would be? How is this different from the Northwest Coast Indians?
2. Find out about a christening party held when a baby gets its name. Compare this to a potlatch. How are they similar? How do they differ?
3. Do we ever use gifts to make people think that we are important? When we give gifts do we ever expect the other person to give us a bigger gift in return?
4. Write a story of a potlatch. Try to write it as if you were a young person in a Northwest Coast tribe, attending your first potlatch. What do you see? How do you feel?

A potlatch was important in establishing a person's position because the people who were invited were witnesses to some important announcement or event. Because the Northwest Coast Indians had no written language, it was necessary to use these large gatherings to let everyone know what was going on. A potlatch might be held to announce a wedding, the completion of a new house or pole, to remind other tribes of control over fishing or hunting grounds, or to celebrate a victory. The songs and chants were records of these important events. In this way, the people of the Northwest Coast were able to keep a record of their history to pass on to their children.

5. A potlatch ensured the legal transfer of names, power, and rights to things like fishing grounds. The people who attended were witnesses. Do we use witnesses when we make legal transfers? Why is having witnesses so important?
6. Ask a lawyer how our ancestors kept legal records before they had writing.

Did You Know?

The Nootka of Vancouver Island called these feasts Tloo-qwah-nah. Europeans named them potlatches. The word "potlatch" comes either from the Nootka word pa-chitla, meaning "to give," or from pa-chuka, "a gift."

Potlatches became bigger and more important after Europeans reached the Northwest Coast. Among some tribes potlatching became a substitute for war. A potlatch could be used to bankrupt enemy tribes and gain prestige. Potlatches became so frequent that missionaries and Indian agents tried to have them stopped. The Indian Act of 1884 outlawed potlatches and some winter dances.

Masked Kwakiutl dancer

The real potlatch, before the whites came, was very different from the modern feast. There were rules to govern every move. These were strictly followed. The feasting lasted for about three months. There was no cash in those days — all gifts were of goods, mostly furs. The wisest and best speakers were chosen to give lectures to those attending the feast. These lectures taught them to respect themselves to honour their chiefs. Young people were told to lead pure lives and to avoid evil. Everyone went home feeling that they had received help and encouragement. But alas! How different today's Potlatch is! It is the root all evil and the big mountain of sin against which missionaries have to fight.

Rev. William H. Pierce, missionary

When I was young, I saw streams of blood shed in war. But since that time, the white men have come and stopped that stream of blood with wealth. Now we fight with our wealth.

Kwakiul elder (1895)

This Indian festival is a debauchery of the worst kind. It is abolutely necessary to put this practice down. At these gatherings they give away their guns and all their property and even so far as to give away their wives.

Sir John A. Macdonald (1884)

To the Superintendent General
of Indian Affairs
Ottawa

Sir,
I have explained to the- tribes the law issued to stop the potlatch. They reply: "It is hard to try and stop us. The white man gives feasts for his friends and goes to the theatres. We have only our dances and potlatches for amusement. We work for our money and like to spend it as we please. We like to gather our friends together and give them food to eat. When we give blankets or money, we sing and dance and all are good friends together. Now, whenever we travel we find friends. The Potlatch does that." There are no doubt evils connected with large gatherings of Indians but they are perfectly satisfied with their way of life. It is hard to make them understand the advantage of giving up the Potlatch or the justice of making them do so.

I have the honour to be, Sir,
Your obedient servant,

Harry Guillod, Indian Agent (1884)

1. One person says: "All are good friends together." Another says: "We fight with our wealth." Can you explain?
2. Potlatches became bigger and were held more often after the Europeans reached the Northwest Coast. Suggest some reasons why.
3. Why do you think some missionaries and Indian Agents wanted to ban the potlatch? Do you think they understood it?
4. Do you think the government was right to ban the potlatch?

Coppers

The most valuable thing a Northwest Coast Indian could own was a copper. Only the very richest people could own of these—a copper could be worth as much as 3000 blankets. Each copper had its own name and history— who had owned it, when it had been bought and sold, how much it was worth. Here is a list of some of the coppers owned by people at Fort Rupert in 1893.

Maxtsolem: *all other coppers are ashamed to look at it,*
7500 blankets
Laxolamas: *steelhead salmon (because it slips out of one's hands like a salmon),*
6000 blankets
Lopelila: *making the house empty of blankets,*
5000 blankets
Dentalayo: *about whose possession all are quarrelling*
Mauaka: *sea lion*
Qauloma: *beaver face*
Leita: *looking below (to find enough blankets to buy it)*
Nenqemala: *bear face*
Kana: *crow*
Qoayim: *whale*
Wina: *war (against the blankets of the purchaser)*

Did You Know?

The first coppers were probably quite small. They came from small pieces of native copper, which were hammered into the shape of small nails or rivets and used as a form of money. After the Europeans came, copper was more easily obtained. The Europeans used large sheets of copper to protect the wooden hulls of their ships from worms. The Indians acquired these sheets and made them into the great coppers like the one held by the chief in the picture.

1. Find Fort Rupert on a map. Locate it on the map on pages 12-13. What people would probably be living there?
2. What do the names of the coppers suggest about (a) how they are decorated and (b) their cost?
3. What do we mean by native copper? Find out where the Indians obtained native copper.
4. Make a replica of a copper using heavy foil. Get your art teacher to help. Choose a name that fits your design.

Bob Harris's Potlatch

"Here's an interesting picture," said Rose. "This potlatch given by a famous carver named Bob Harris at Alert Bay in 1910."

"1910?" said Paul in surprise. "I thought you said it was against the law."

"Yes it was," replied Rose, "but the potlatch was very important to our culture, and many people kept it up in secret, especially among the Kwakiutl. We have records of potlatches in the 1920s and 1930s, though it was dying out by then."

"Gee," said Paul, "that's not so long ago. My grandma and grandpa are always talking about those days."

"Yes," agreed Rose. "Don't forget that ours is a living culture. We've been in contact with European culture for about 200 years. Almost everything has changed somehow, but it has adapted without dying out. In fact, we can follow the story of how things have changed over the years."

1. Look up Alert Bay in your atlas. Locate it on the map on pages 12-13. What people would be living there?
2. Why might it be possible to have a potlatch there even though it was against the law?
3. Look at the picture. What kinds of

Mr. and Mrs. Harris in ceremonial costume

things are being given away at the potlatch? What other signs of European influence can you find?

Did You Know

The most spectacular thing a Northwest Coast Indian could do to prove that he was very rich was to "break" a copper at a potlatch. "Breaking" a copper meant cutting pieces off it until only the T-shaped ridge was left.

4. Look at the copper Mrs. Harris is holding How many times has it been broken?

Europeans did not come to the Northwest Coast until quite late, compared to the rest of the New World. Francis Drake may have visited the area over 400 years ago, but it is unlikely that he came that far north. The Spanish explored the coast of California in 1602-3, but did not reach the Northwest either.

It was the Russians who arrived first. They came from Siberia in the 1730s and 1740s. They traded for sea otter furs along the coast of Alaska, but it was some years before they made a settlement. Next came the Spanish, who sent several expeditions up the coast from their colonies in Mexico during the 1750s and 1760s. They reached Vancouver Island and the Queen Charlottes but made only temporary camps.

In 1778 the famous British explorer Captain James Cook sailed along the coast from Oregon to Alaska. He stopped for a month at Nootka Sound to repair his ship and trade for furs. Captain George Vancouver followed in 1791. He discovered the Strait of Georgia and finished the surveys and mapping that Cook had started.

In 1793 Alexander Mackenzie, the Canadian explorer and fur trader, became the first person to reach the coast overland from the east. His journey ended at Bella Coola. In 1805 the Americans Lewis and Clark also reached the Pacific overland by travelling down the Columbia River.

Something to Do

Work in groups to learn more about some of the explorers who visited the Northwest Coast, such as; Vitus Bering; Juan Perez, Bruno Heceta and Juan Francisco de Bodega y Quadra; James Cook and George Vancouver; Alexander Mackenzie, Simon Fraser, David Thompson; Meriwether Lewis and William Clark. Each group might report its findings to the class and prepare a bulletin board display using maps and pictures.

The Fur Trade

"It was Captain Cook's voyage that changed things most for the Indians," explained Rose. "Cook's ships stopped in Canton on the way home and some of his men sold the furs they had got at Nootka Sound. Sea otter furs were highly prized by rich merchants in China. The sailors made incredible profits, and when the news got out trading ships flocked to the Northwest Coast to buy sea otter furs.

"The Indians actually did well for themselves in the fur trade. It was a seller's market. They soon learned to get a good price and they only took things they wanted. Some traders had very unhappy times. Here's what happened to Captain Charles Bishop when he tried to trade with the Chinook in 1795:"

"We expected that with the choice goods that compose our cargo, we should have been able to procure furs with ease, but after bartering and showing them a great variety of articles for the whole day we did not purchase a single fur. Tea Kettles, sheet Copper, a variety of fine cloths and in short the most valuable articles of our Cargo were shown without producing the desired effect, and in the evening the whole of them took to their canoes, and paddled to the shore, leaving us not more disappointed than surprized.

"The next day the natives began to set their own Price on the Skins, which was not moderate. On the third day, we broke trade, but not at the prices we wanted."

1. According to Captain Bishop's journal, what trade goods did he offer the Indians?
2. What do you think the Indians would do with these things?
3. What other things might the Indians ask for?

Far and away the most important trade item was metal. Sometimes the Indians asked for tools, pots and pans, knives, or other finished products. But often they wanted raw metal and traders brought shiploads of iron slabs, called "toes," that the Indians could shape any way they wanted. Other trade items were guns, gunpowder and ammunition, buttons, beads, cloth and clothing, pots, pans, kettles, blankets, and tobacco.

Something to Do

1. You are a cabin boy on the brig Adventure trading with the Bella Coola in 1798. Write a letter to your parents telling about the arrrival of your ship in the first Bella Coola village. What did the sailors think when they saw the village and the strange customs of the Indians?
2. Write and perform a play about the first meeting between Indians and traders in a Bella Coola village.
3. You are a young Bella Coola boy or girl in 1798. Make up a song or chant about the arrival of the first trading ship in your village. You will sing this song during the winter feasts. It will tell guests from other villages about the ship and the strange customs of the white traders.

The Trading Companies

The great days of the sea otter trade were over very quickly. By 1800 the animals were almost extinct from over-trapping, and fewer and fewer ships made the voyage to the Northwest. In their place came the big fur-trading companies — the Northwest Company and the Hudson's Bay Company. Instead of making a quick visit in a ship and then moving on, these traders came by land and built permanent trading posts. During the 1820s, 30s and 40s the Hudson's Bay Company set up a series of posts, from Fort Vancouver on the Columbia River to Forts Stikine and Taku on southern Alaska.

The British, the Russians, the Americans, and the Spanish all claimed parts of the coast, but in the early days this did not affect the Indians. There were no settlers, miners or loggers to take the land away. The only outsiders were the fur traders, who stayed close to their forts leaving the Indians to do as they pleased.

1. Make a list of the HBC posts that were built on the coast and locate them on the map on pages 12-13. Why would the company choose these places?
2. The Bay was a British company. How did it come to have posts in Alaska and Oregon?

Did You Know

Blankets were such an important trade item that they came to be used as money. The value of something was the number of blankets it was worth.

1. If the average price of a trade blanket was approximately $1.50 during the nineteenth century, what would be the value of the coppers listed on page 50?

"Here's a challenge for you Paul," said Rose. "Let's see how good you are at making logical guesses. What do you think would happen to the Indians' way of life as a result of all these goods? How do you think their culture would change?

"Well," said Paul (thinking very fast), "I guess, ug, if they had metal tools they could hunt and fish more easily. Their standard of living probably got better. I suppose they'd have more food, or the same amount of food for less work. Cooking would be easier with metal pots. And they wouldn't have to spend all that time making cedar bark clothing if they could get cloth from the traders."

"Yes, you're absolutely right," said Rose.

"The fur trade made the people richer, and it also gave them more leisure. So what do you think they would do next?"

"Oh gee. Well, if I'd been them I would have tried to improve my house — put in stoves, chimneys, windows with glass, a proper floor — things like that. Maybe scrap my canoe and get a proper boat with sails and decks."

"Now you're way off the track," said Rose. "The Indians took the new tools but they used them in their own way. Iron made it much easier to cut down trees and carve wood, but the carvings, the houses, the canoes, the bowls and chests were all done in the traditional style.

The Haida village of Skidegate around 1878

"One of the big changes was in art. As far as we can tell, the totem poles began to get bigger and the masks more detailed and elaborate soon after the traders arrived. The new tools were the main reason, but there was something else that helped the Indian artists. Can you guess what it might be?

"Was it the copper plates — the ones from the hulls of the ships?"

"That's a very good answer, and you're quite right," said Rose , "but I'm thinking of something else — paint and dyes."

"Didn't they already have them?"

"Yes, but the natural colours were very dull compared to the trade goods and, just like people anywhere, the Indians like their designs to be nice and bright. The hundred years after the first contact with Europeans was the golden age of Northwest Coast culture."

1. Look up the word catalyst in your dictionary. Use your own words to tell what it means. Ask your teacher for help if you are not sure.

2. Contact with European traders was a catalyst for Northwest Coast Indian culture. What does this statement mean? Do you agree or disagree? Explain.

3. What other changes do you think would take place as a result of contact with the traders?

A coming-of-age ceremony for Kwakiutl boy

The Rivalry Potlach

"What about the potlach?" suggested Rose,

"Well…" thought Paul, "I guess if the people became richer, there would be more stuff to give away. The potlaches probably got bigger — or maybe they had them more often."

"Yes, and the character of the potlach began to change, too. Remember how a person's importance was measured by wealth? Well, suppose an ordinary person turned out to be a very good trapper and a very good bargainer in the fur trade. He might become as rich as the hereditary chief, or richer.

"Before the Europeans arrived there was almost no chance of this, but afterwards it sometimes happened that people of low status became rich. The newly-rich person would use his wealth to give a potlach just like the traditional chiefs — it would prove how rich he was, and would make him respected and important in the village,"

1. What do the words *traditional* and *heredity* mean? Look them up in your dictionary. Make up definitions using your own words.
2. The Indians of the Northwest Coast had a *traditional* society ruled by hereditary chiefs. What does this mean? Do you agree?
3. How might contact with European society change this?
4. Do we have traditions today? Do we inherit things in our society?

"Here's another reason," continued Rose. "When a trading post was built, the people from nearby villages would often move there to be close to the trade goods. Before, each chief had been the head of his own village. Now, he was only one chief among, perhaps, a dozen. The chiefs had to work out who would be head chief in the new larger village. Potlaching was how they did it.

"We call these rivalry potlatches, and once people started competing with one another it became a vicious circle. You couldn't stop without admitting you were defeated, and losing your status and importance. Here's a story about one of these potlatches."

A Kwakuitl potlach story

A powerful Kwakuitl chief sent invitations for a potlach to tribes all along the coast. To impress his guests, the chief turned tables piled high with fish and berries over into a blazing fore. He poured barrels of valuable oolachan oil over the flames. Then he snapped his fingers and said: "Hah, that is how much I care about food and oil! I have plenty to spare."

Next it was the turn of a visiting chief to see what he could do. He attempted to put out the fire by covering it with a huge copper worth 8000 blankets.

To match his guest, the host had five men drag five canoes into the longhouse. These canoes were chopped into pieces and thrown on the fire. The host announced that these canoes were each worth 5000 blankets.

The rival chief had come prepared. He had brought with him 400 blankets. He ordered his men to throw these blankets onto the fire.

The host had more canoes chopped up to keep the dying fire going. But even that was not enough to satisfy him. He tore down a section of his own house and threw the wood on the fire.

The guest chief could not match this last act. He left, hoping to rebuild his fortune. Then he would entertain his host with a bigger and better potlach.

The host chief had lost all his wealth. Even part of his house was gone. But now he had another name — House Burner — to add to his other honours. His tribe was proud of him and would sing songs about his potlach.

Did You Know?

A copper usually doubled in value every time it was sold. By the early years of the twentieth century the great rivalry potlaches had made some coppers so valuable no one could afford to buy them. Sometimes several men formed a partnership because no one person had enough.

Rivalry potlatches sometimes became very bitter, even dangerous. In 1935, a potlatch given by the Owikeno people of Rivers Inlet became so violent that the entire village caught fire and burned to the ground, leaving the people destitute.

1. Find rivers Inlet in an atlas or on a road map of British Columbia. What people would the Owikeno have been a part of?
2. Suggest reasons why the Owikeno were still potlaching as recently as the 1930s.

MISSIONARIES AND SCHOOLS

From about the middle of the nineteenth century missionaries began to come to the Northwest Coast. They went to live with the Indian people and tried to convert them to Christianity. The missionaries attacked the old beliefs. To convert the peopel to Christianity they had to stop the Indian religion. They had persuaded the government to ban the potlach and other ceremonies that kept the old ways alive. Sometimes they burned the totem poles and destroyed or confiscated the masks and rattles that were important to the Indian religion. The Northwest Coast Indians were very spiritual people. Many came to believe in the new religion.

Some missionaries wanted the Indians to give up their old way of life as well as their religious beliefs. They built schools and the taught people to speak English. Children were punished — sometimes even beaten — if they spoke the Indian languages. These missionaries told the people to wear European-style clothes, build Eurpean style houses, eat European-style food. At the same time, some missionaries tried to protect the Indians from the worst features of the European culture. One such missionary was William Duncan, who came to work among the Tsimshian in 1857.

Indians, particularly in remote areas, kept the old ways alive. The ceremonies wcrc still performed. But now they were conducted in secret because they were against the law.

Reserves, Laws, and Indian Agents

European settlement forced the Indians to give up most of their territories and live on small areas of land that were set aside for them. (In Canada these are called *reserves*, in the United States and in much of Canada the federal governments signed treaties with the Indian peoples. The treaties stated what lands would be given to the Indians, and promised food, homes, protection and money in return for the land that was given up.

Tsimshian children at Metlakatla

In British Columbia, however, no treaties were ever signed. The Indians were given very small reserves to live on, and the land was usually poor. The white settlers took the best lands for themselves. In 1915 much of the best farmland that still belonged to the Indians was cut off the reserves and given to white settlers.

In Alaska, the government caused problems for the Indians by leasing rivers and streams to commercial fishing and canning companies. The companies had exclusive rights to the streams. The Indians were no longer allowed to fish in them even though they had lived there for generations and depended on them for food.

Sechelt Indians practice for a religious pagent, 1901

58

The Indians had to obey laws and regulations imposed by the new governments. Many of these laws were designed to make the Indians change their way of life. At the same time, the Indians did not have the same rights as other people in Canada and the United States. In British Columbia, for example, some missionaries were appointed justices of the peaces by the government. If the people did not do what the missionary wanted he was able to use the power of the law to fine or punish them.

The governments appointed Indian Agents to run the reserves and enforce the laws. Some agents were very active in putting down the old ways. For example, when Daniel Cranmer gave a great potlach in 1922, the Indian Agent, William Halliday, brought criminal charges against 34 of the people who attended it. He took away the masks, rattles, robes and other regalis that were used in the potlach. These were sold to collectors.

These things all made it very difficult for the Indians to keep their culture alive. Over the years many of the old ways were lost. The old Northwest Coast way of life was gone forever. But the Indians found that putting on European clothes, going to church, and speaking English didn't make them the same as other Canadians and Americans. They didn't have the same rights as other people. Many could not vote, enter into contracts, or do many things that citizens of a country take for granted. They faced ignorance and prejudice in schools and on the job. Many could not cope with being out of place in society. Others fought to keep pride alive and improve things for their people.

These Haida men are wearing their best clothes to show that they are chiefs

The New and the Old

"Well," said Rose, "that brings the story up to the present, It's hard to describe how things are for the Northwest Coast Indians nowadays, because condtions are so different from place to place and group to group. Some Indians live in the heart of Vancouver, while others live in tiny villages on isolated fjords up the coast.

"However, there are two things that seem to be happening: First, most of the native people seem to have adapted to the North American culture. Second, there is growing revival of interest in the old ways and a growing demand for recognition of Indain rights.

"This creates a great challenge. On the one hand, we know we have to change and adapt to the modern world. On the other, we want to keep our separate identity as Indians, and we want to preserve our cultural heritage. Norhtwest Coast Indian people are trying to combine the new ways with the old."

Did You Know

When the Canadian Indian Act was revised in 1951, the ban on the potlatch was dropped. Potlatches have been legal since then.

Trees and fish were the basis of the Northwest Coast Indian life in the old days, and today they are still the two most important industries along the coast in Alaska and British Columbia. Many native people are employed in these industries, especially fishing, as the methods of fishing have changed the Indians have changed too. Modern trawlers and seiners with deisel engines have replaced dugout canoes and fish traps. Along the coast in towns like Tahsis, Port Alberni, Prince Rupert, Bella Coola and Uclllueeelet, fleets of native-owned fishing boats fill the harbours. Native fishermen have organized their own union. One native band runs its own fish canning plant.

Northwest Coast Indains continue to cut trees in British Columbia's forests. Some bands, such as the Niska of the Nass Valley, have forest lands on their reserves. These bands have their own logging companies. Native people also work in the sawmills along the coast.

Several coastal bands run their own businesses. A band in North Vancouver has a busy marina on its land. Park Royal, a big shopping centre, is on reserve land. The band rents the land to the shopping centre. Other native-owned businesses include tourist facilities and mobile home parks. Native people are taking part in politics. In recent years Frank Clader and Frank Howard have been elected to the British legislature with support from native and non-native voters alike.

Native people are also making strong claims for their rights. Land claims are an important issue in British Columbia. Before the First World War the Niska (Nishga) petitioned the government for a fair land settlement, but their petition was rejected. In recent years other tribes have demanded that the government

A Bella Coola fisherman mends his net

Modern logging methods

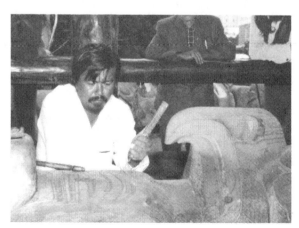

A carver at work

give back the masks, rattles, carvings and other treasures that were taken away.

There has been a revival of native art. Masks, rattles, dishes, headpieces and other traditional carvings are now being made again. Fortunately the skills of the native artists have not been lost, and the modern carvings are as beautiful and striking as the old ones were. Native artists are exploring new techniques such as silver work and silkscreen prints on paper.

Near Hazelton on the Skeena River, the Gitskan people have built a cultural centre in the form of a traditional Northwest Coast village. It is called K'san, which means "breath of our fathers." K'san has become a place where Indian artists from many different groups can come together to study, work, and carry on the traditions of the Northwest Coast.

In universities in Washington, British Columbia, and Alaska young Northwest Coast Indian people deal with the modern world. Some are learning skills to help their people deal with the modern world. Some are learning to be lawyers, to help deal with land claims and other legal issues. At both Simon Fraser University and the University of British Columbia, special programs have been set up to train Indian teachers. In community schools at places such as Bella Coola and Mt. Currie, adults and children alike learn both the old ways and languages, and the new. The Indians of the Northwest Coast are reviving the old ways in many areas. Potlatches are being held again. The old dances and ceremonies have come out of their secret hiding places.

Did You Know?

The treasures that were taken away after Daniel Cranmer's potlatch are being retured to the Lekwiltok people. A special museum was opened in 1979 at Cape Mudge to house them.

The Lekwiltok are Christians now. On the day the museum opened they first held a service in their village church. Then they put on their masks and costumes to perform the ancient cedar-bark ceremony, and a dance of welcome for the return of their long-lost treasures.

Raising a pole at K'san

Ms. Sailor led Paul to the last in the series of bulletin boards. This one had its title "First Nations People Today". On it were several colourful posters celebrating the achievements of native peopel in a variety of fields: among them ice hockey, theatre, motion pictures, clothing design, law, business, and traditional arts. Here, too, were newspaper and magazine articles telling students from the Bella Coola area who had just graduated from the University of British Columbia and who were planning to return to the north coast to teach.

Paul was impressed. "I had no idea that native people were doing so many different things."

"You are not alone, Paul," replied Ms. Sailor. "Very few Canadians have any idea of the fact that native people today are enjoying success in many areas. But don't let these 'success' stories fool you; there are still many difficult challenges facing our people today. And, not everyone would agree that these are the measures of achievement for first nations people."

Idea for Discussion:

Many first nations peoples regard individual achievement as being less important than actions or activites which benefit the whole of one's family, community, or people. Consider how life in your school or community might be different if this approach to life were followed.

Ms. Sailor pointed to a series of articles clipped from recent newspapers and magazines displayed on the bulletin board. Paul read their titles: "Native youths find jobs scarce both on the reserve and in the city"; "Land claims case goes to Supreme Court"; "Native fishermen gain rights on Skeena River"; "Native fight for self-government goes on despite constitutional set-back"; "Local Indian band demands say in forest management".

Sample "exerpts" from articles on the bulletin board:

Native Youths find jobs scarce both on the reserve and in the city

Unemployment rates on Indian reserves are two to three times as great as in other B.C. communities and economic opportunities limited in most areas. Hardest hit are the young people who often have to leave the reserve and their families to find work. Once in the city, however, they often find that their chances of getting a job are a little better than at home. Often, the native young people find that they haven't the education or skills needed for the jobs that are available...

Land claims case goes to Supreme Court

...band has launched an action in the Supreme Court of British Columbia seeking to gain control over an area of nearly 150 000 hectares of northwestern B.C. which the natives claim as their traditional homeland. A spokesperson for the band council said: "We have been trying for more than a decade to reach a negotiated settlement with the government but have had no success so we are forced to turn to the courts..."

Native Fishermen gain rights on Skeena River

New fishing regulations will allow local native bands to sell "food" fish caught in the Skeena River. While native leaders hailed the decision as a restoration of their traditional rights, non-native fishermen were angered by a move that they see as meaning fewer fish for them form an already declining catch.

Native fight for self-government goes on despite constitutional set-back

The failure of the 1992 Charlottetown Constitutional Accord does not mean that the fight for native self-government is dead. B.C. native leaders have hailed the recent finding of the Royal Commission on Aboriginal Issues that Canada's native peoples already have the constitutional right to self-government. This interpretation of the aboriginal rights section of the constitution, announced by Royal Commission co-chair George Erasmus at a recent press conference, was immediately challenged by some legal experts...

Local Indian band demands say in forest management

Native communities should play a role in forest management decisions. That's the position put forward by local band members in a brief submitted to the provincial government. Citing land claims, traditional relationships with the land and its resources, and the economic concerns of native peoples, the report calls upon the provincial government to give local native bands greater control over forestry operations and practices in the region.

"All of these stories deal with the struggles first nations peoples face in Canada today. The issues are all pretty much the same, whether they are in Quebec, or in the Arctic, or here on the Pacific Coast: the system under which our lives have been governed for more then a century has not worked and needs to be changed."

"You see, Paul, under the terms of the *Indian Act*, first nations peoples were treated very differently than other Canadians. All aspects of our lives were controlled by the federal government. We had lost nearly all of our land and placed on reserves; we could not make decisions about our education, health care, or other important areas; we couldn't even vote in elections for nearly 100 years after we became "Canadians". Our lives were run by the Department of Indian Affairs. Today, the first nations want to establish a new relationship with the federal and provincial governments, one that would give us greater control over our own lives after so many years of being controlled by Ottawa.

"There are many things we would like to see happen but two stand out as very important at this time: land claims and native self-government. Here in British Columbia there are almost no treaties between the first nations and the provincail or federal governments; our lands were simply taken from us and our people placed on reserves. Native peoples have tried to negotiate with the government regarding these claims but most often they have ended up going before the courts — which is a costly and time-consuming process. The Gitk'san, for example, have had their case before the courts for more than ten years now and it still drags on. Land claims are important to us. On a more practical level, restoration

of our our traditional lands would improve our economic situation and help end the cycle of poverty that has been so common on reserves in Canada.

"Native self-government is also an important issue for first nations peoples. In simple terms it means gaining control over our own affairs and being able to make decisions for ourselves that other governments have made for far too long. Some progress has been made in this area. The native peoples of Canada's far north now enjoy the ability to make most of the decisions affecting their lives. On a smaller scale, here in British Columbia, the Sechelt nation operates its own local government and the Nish'ga have control over their own district. What our people want, however, is a constitutional recognition of our right to govern ourselves on our own lands according to the traditions and needs of our peoples."

Paul thought for a moment. "Things are sure more complicated than they were in the old villages, aren't they Ms. Sailor," he said.

"They are indeed, Paul," his teacher answered. "We can't go back to the old days; we can only try to make things better for our people today and for our children and grandchildren in the near future."